A PLUME BOOK

LESSONS FROM A DOG

Photo by Erica Gorochow

Patrick Moberg is an illustrator. He lives in New York.

LESSONS
FROM A DOG

PATRICK MOBERG

A PLUME BOOK

PLUME
Published by the Penguin Group
Penguin Group (USA) LLC
375 Hudson Street
New York, New York 10014

USA | Canada | UK | Ireland | Australia | New Zealand | India | South Africa | China
penguin.com
A Penguin Random House Company
First published by Plume, a member of Penguin Group (USA) LLC, 2014

REGISTERED TRADEMARK — MARCA REGISTRADA

LIBRARY OF CONGRESS CATALOGING-IN-PUBLICATION DATA

Moberg, Patrick, author.
Lessons from a dog / Patrick Moberg.
pages   cm
ISBN 978-0-14-218133-1 (hardback)
1. Dogs — Humor. I. Title.
SF426.2.M63 2014
636.7 — dc23   2014018775

Printed in the United States of America

1   3   5   7   9   10   8   6   4   2

DEDICATED TO BURTON, NEMO,
FRIDA, WALTER AND PETEY

LESSONS FROM A DOG

SOMETIMES THE BEST ADVICE...

COMES FROM UNEXPECTED SOURCES.

GIVE AND ACCEPT AFFECTION. FREELY AND OFTEN.

BE CURIOUS ABOUT THE
WORLD AROUND YOU.
ESPECIALLY WHEN NEW
PEOPLE COME INTO IT.

WHEN SOMEONE PREPARES

FOOD FOR YOU, DEVOUR IT

LIKE IT'S THE BEST MEAL

YOU'VE EVER EATEN.

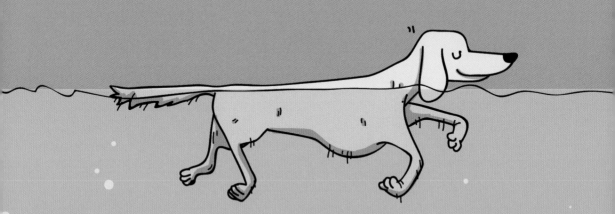

GET DIRTY.

ACCIDENTS HAPPEN.

A FRIENDLY SMILE
CAN WORK WONDERS.

DON'T BE AFRAID TO ASK FOR HELP FROM FRIENDS.

BUT BE WILLING TO CHANGE YOUR MIND.

PROTECT THE ONES YOU LOVE.

DEVELOP AN APPRECIATION FOR THE ABSURD.

AND, IF YOU'RE REALLY
PASSIONATE, DON'T LET
THAT STOP YOU.

LET YOUR
FRIENDS KNOW
WHEN YOU'VE
MISSED THEM.

LOOK AT A
PROBLEM FROM
ALL ANGLES.

WHEN YOU CAN MAKE SOMEONE'S
LIFE A LITTLE EASIER, DO...

BUT DON'T LET THEM
TAKE ADVANTAGE OF YOU.

DIFFERENT BREEDS...

AREN'T ALL THAT DIFFERENT.

MAKE TIME FOR FUN EVERY DAY.

ENJOY LIFE'S LUXURIES...

BUT REMEMBER IT'S JUST STUFF.

DON'T HIDE YOUR EXCITEMENT.

TEST YOUR LIMITS.

BE PATIENT WITH LITTLE ONES.

TAKE NAPS.

LEARN NEW TRICKS.

YOU HAVE TO EARN A LIFE OFF THE LEASH.

CUDDLE.

BREATHE AND LOOK AROUND.

FORGIVE FRIENDS
WHO DON'T HAVE
TIME TO PLAY.

GO OUT OF YOUR
WAY WHEN THEY DO.

WHEN YOU ARE GONE,

YOU WILL BE MISSED.